The Little Book of

ACT

A Simple and Fun Guide to
Living a Meaningful Life Using
Acceptance and Commitment Therapy

Shamash Alidina

Dedication

This book is dedicated to all the individuals who have generously supported and encouraged me in sharing Acceptance and Commitment Therapy (ACT) and mindfulness. Your belief in my vision has been the cornerstone of this endeavour – you know who you are, and I am profoundly thankful for each one of you.

I extend this dedication to Steven C. Hayes, the originator of ACT, and to all who have enriched the ACT movement. Your dedication has cultivated a legacy from which we all benefit, and for which we owe much gratitude.

To my readers, may this book serve as a guide and a companion on your journey towards mindfulness, compassion, wisdom and acceptance.

With peace and love,
Shamash

About the Author

Shamash Alidina has been a mindfulness teacher for over 20 years. Since 2013 he's been training mindfulness teachers in programmes that are fully online. And over the last few years, he's grown a huge passion for Acceptance and Commitment Therapy (ACT). He's studied ACT through programmes by Dr Steven C. Hayes, Dr Russ Harris, Dr Joe Oliver and many others.

Shamash is the author of nine books on mindfulness, including the international bestseller, *Mindfulness For Dummies.*

Shamash publishes insights, blogs and videos every week which he shares with his email subscribers and offers a range of online courses and coaching in ACT and mindfulness teacher training. He offers a live meditation daily in his Daily Mindfulness Club. He supports mindfulness and ACT teachers in a community called Teach Mindfulness Academy. He helps people publish books through his Mindful Book Publishing program. And he supports mindfulness and ACT teachers to find more work through his Mindful Business Inner Circle program.

To find out more:
Free ACT Course: shamashalidina.com/act-book
Web: shamashalidina.com
Email: info@shamashalidina.com

Social Media
Instagram: @shamashalidina
YouTube: @shamashmindful
TikTok: @shamashalidina
LinkedIn: @shamashalidina
Facebook: @shamashalidina
X: @shamashalidina

Table of Contents

How to Use This Book

Hello and welcome to this short introduction to ACT. Thank you so much for choosing this book. I feel honoured to join you on your journey into this subject.

I've made some assumptions in this book. I'm assuming you're new to ACT (which stands for Acceptance and Commitment Therapy or Acceptance and Commitment Training). Maybe you're having (or considering having) some therapy or coaching based on ACT. Or perhaps you're a practitioner exploring how to bring this approach into your work. You may even be someone into mindfulness and wondering what all this ACT stuff is about. Whoever you are, I hope you find this book a helpful introduction.

This book is deliberately written as a short and simple introduction to ACT. Having read lots of books on ACT myself, I realised that most of them go into great depth. I personally love very short and simple introductions to new subjects and so I wanted to create such a book for you.

Although this book is short, I've tried to ensure it includes all the key aspects of ACT. If you want to learn more about ACT after taking your time to read and digest what I've shared, there are many other excellent books and resources that go into the subject in greater depth, and I share some of these at the end of this book.

A note about language. I use the words *thoughts* and *feelings* in this book a lot. When I say thoughts, I am referring to the words, images and memories that pop up in your head. When I say feelings, I am referring to your emotions, bodily sensations and urges.

You'll find this book balances ACT theory with stories, metaphors and practical exercises. The stories and metaphors are labelled with an icon, so you can spot them easily when flicking through the book. Each chapter introduces a theoretical concept and then shares a related story or metaphor, one that is designed to bring the theory to life. Most of the metaphors I have developed are unique, to help enrich your reading experience and deepen your understanding of the ideas, even if you've read other books on ACT.

There are three parts to the book. Part 1 provides an overview of ACT; Part 2 teaches some ways you can put ACT into practice and Part 3 shares some ways you can integrate ACT into your everyday life.

I think you'll find this book makes more sense if you read it in the order it's written. But feel free to dip in and out of the chapters if you wish. You may also find it helpful to refer back to this book after you've read it, perhaps to revisit the practical ACT exercises in Part 2 and Part 3, or to remind yourself of some of the key concepts or stories.

Trying the ACT exercises is an important part of getting the most out of this book. I can explain why using the example of running. Running is an excellent form of exercise for some people but reading about running just isn't the same. Reading this book is a bit like reading a description of how to run. It's important to know how to run, what others say about running, and how to train effectively. But after some reading, the best way to experience running is to get up and go for a run. That's the only way to reap the benefits of running.

In the same way, the best way to experience ACT and its benefits is to try the ACT exercises. Ideally do them several times a day for several weeks. You'll then notice the benefits and understand the concepts more deeply. The combination of reading, reflecting and trying out the various exercises is what I would recommend.

Look out for these exercises (labelled 'ACT Exercise') in Part 2 and Part 3 of this book.

In this book, I introduce you to just a small selection of the many ACT exercises that are possible. So, if you don't find the particular exercises in this book helpful but you like the idea of ACT, do explore other books and courses to try more exercises. There are literally hundreds you can try!

I've included some light-hearted jokes throughout this book, labelled with an icon. If you're going through a tough time, jokes may be the last thing on your mind. But I just couldn't help it. I love 'bad jokes'. Feel free to ignore them if you wish – I totally understand and apologise in advance!

I've found ACT to be really helpful in my own life, helping me to step out of limiting beliefs and take action to do things I find more meaningful. I've also found the practitioners (therapists, coaches and teachers) I've trained say they find the approach personally appealing, and they find it helps their clients too.

However, before I get too excited, let's remember that ACT isn't for everyone. No one therapy or coaching approach is. So, I encourage you to read the book and try out the practical exercises, and work with a therapist if you feel you need to. But if you really don't find ACT helpful, you're not the only one. There are many other alternative therapies or coaching approaches available that you can try instead.

With that, I wish to thank you for choosing to begin your ACT journey with me, and I look forward to walking alongside you on this journey. If you're ready to begin exploring, let's go for it!

Part 1

Understanding ACT

In this part, you'll discover what ACT is, how it's different from other therapeutic approaches, and some of the benefits of ACT. You'll also get a simple overview of the purpose of ACT and lots of stories to help you understand how ACT works.

1.

What is ACT?

ACT is designed for everyone. When it's used therapeutically, it stands for Acceptance and Commitment Therapy. When it's used in other settings, it stands for Acceptance and Commitment Training. It's a well-tested approach based on over 40 years of scientific research that offers practical and creative ways to thrive, and it helps you navigate through the challenges you face in modern life.

The aim of ACT is to help you create a life that's rich, meaningful and hopefully enjoyable too. So, if you feel your life is lacking in meaning, or you're finding yourself getting overwhelmed by your thoughts or feelings, ACT could be ideal for you.

ACT helps you flourish by improving what is called your *psychological flexibility*. Psychological flexibility may sound a bit confusing. But at its essence it's very simple. It's the ability to do what matters most to you in your everyday life and flexibly navigate through any unhelpful thoughts and difficult feelings that come up along the way.

The more psychological flexibility you have, the more meaningful your life will be and the less you will feel tangled up with your thoughts and feelings. That's ultimately what most of us want. So, how do you increase this psychological flexibility?

ACT has discovered there are only six skills you need to learn to develop more psychological flexibility. These are called *flexibility skills* (you will find out more about these six skills in Part 2). The good news is that many of the exercises in this book will improve several of these skills at the same time.

People who have developed high levels of psychological flexibility have been found, in over 3,000 studies, to live healthy and fulfilling lives. And because it's developed using skills that you can practise, you can work on improving your psychological flexibility too. It's considered by many leading psychologists to be the key factor that determines whether you live a flourishing and meaningful life.

Psychological flexibility is a super skill for your physical, mental, emotional and spiritual health.

Once you learn to develop the six flexibility skills, you can integrate them into your life however you wish. Use the techniques that work for you to get you moving towards a fulfilling life. You can even make up your own unique exercises once you understand the six skills.

So, in essence, ACT seeks to help you relate to your challenges in a radically different way, so life has greater purpose and you can enjoy greater peace of mind.

ACT isn't just for overcoming mental health challenges for individuals. ACT is also great when applied in schools, work, prisons, local communities and for any individual. This is because greater psychological flexibility is beneficial for everyone, from children to teachers to refugees to corporate executives to Olympic athletes. Yes, Olympic athletes have used ACT to help them achieve gold medals. So, who knows what you'll achieve or who you'll be able to help with these skills over the long term!

METAPHOR The Flexible Gardener

Imagine your mind is like a garden. In this garden, each plant and flower stands for your thoughts and feelings. The bright flowers and tasty vegetables are the good parts of life — the happy thoughts and the things you do that make you feel proud. But, just like any garden, there are also weeds. These weeds are the worries, fears, and sad feelings that pop up sometimes. If you're like many other people, you may have lots of weeds and are frustrated by them.

You might think that to have a nice garden, you need to pull out all these weeds and throw them away. But pulling weeds is hard, and they seem to come back in force even when you try to get rid of them. Some of the weeds are prickly, and you're scared to even touch them. Other weeds seem to spread everywhere, even in your best flowerbeds. But the truth is, weeds are a normal part of a garden, just like tough times are a normal part of life.

In ACT, you learn to let the weeds be. You don't let them take over, but you also don't spend all your time trying to fight them. Instead, you pay more attention to the flowers and vegetables — the parts that matter. You take care of these by watering them, making sure they get enough sun, and enjoying their colours and smells. This means you're choosing to focus on what's meaningful for you, even though the weeds are still there.

Sometimes, the weeds might grow a lot and mix in with your flowers. It might seem a bit messy, but that's okay. It doesn't mean your garden is ruined. It means you're doing what all good gardeners do — looking after the plants that are important to you, no matter what else is growing around them.

You may even begin to see the beauty of the weeds. You realise that 'weeds' are just a label – a story that you tell yourself. Weeds are not really weeds – they are just plants that we don't want. And over time, you may even enjoy them in their own, unique way.

Your garden will change with the seasons. Flowers will bloom and then fade away, and new ones will come up. This shows that your garden — and your life — is always changing, and that's something beautiful, not something to worry about. Your garden doesn't have to be perfect without any weeds. It's a special place where you can learn to be okay with everything that grows, the good and the not-so-good. This is what ACT is all about — finding peace with all parts of life.

2.

What ACT is Not

ACT does not focus on reducing, fixing or getting rid of your thoughts or feelings. Even the top Master ACT practitioner in the world has difficult thoughts and feelings – it's part of being human.

Instead, ACT teaches you how to *relate* to your thoughts and feelings in a more effective way. By 'effective', I mean in a way that makes your life richer, more fulfilling and, ultimately, more enjoyable too.

When you're suffering from feelings like anxiety or depression, or painful sensations, the natural temptation is to find a way to get rid of them. Some feelings can be annoying at best and feel life-threatening at their worst. Many therapies and coaching approaches focus on trying to get rid of these feelings and thoughts.

ACT takes a radically different approach. It doesn't encourage you to get rid of any thoughts or feelings. Sadly, trying to get rid of tricky thoughts and feelings can just make them stronger and stickier, leading to more issues. Research shows that trying to eliminate such feelings is ineffective and leads to more suffering: the harder you try, the stronger those thoughts and feelings come back and the more you are likely to suffer.

But don't worry, there's lots of hope with ACT! This can be the tricky part to understand, however, as the hope doesn't come from having fewer challenging thoughts and feelings. The hope comes from living a more meaningful life, no matter where your life has taken you. ACT gives you the skills to open up and make space for your inner experiences so you can focus on creating a meaningful life. Every moment is a chance to begin again fresh and take action towards living the life that's most meaningful for you. The idea is you bring your thoughts and feelings with you for the ride.

Once you learn to relate to your thoughts and feelings in a more skilful way and begin focusing on what really matters in your life, you'll probably find your thoughts and feelings don't bother you quite so much. But that's never the aim with ACT – your painful thoughts and feelings can arise as much as they wish, but you become skilled at seeing them for what they are – internal, private experiences that come and go. You get to choose how to live your life, whatever thoughts and feelings happen to arise.

STORY The Monkey That Didn't Let Go

There was once an injured monkey lost in the jungle. The monkey needed treatment, but the vet just couldn't find it. She knew the monkey loved bananas, and then she had a brilliant idea (she must have been reading about ACT!).

She secured an open glass jar to the base of a tree. Inside the jar she put a small banana. Then she waited.

Sure enough, the monkey noticed the banana and came rushing to get it. The monkey put his hand in, grasped the banana, but was then stuck!

He kept trying to get the banana out. But when he created a fist by holding on to the banana, it was impossible for him to get his hand out. The only way out was to let go. But he didn't let go of that banana.

So, he kept fighting and pulling and pushing. The vet found the monkey and was able to give him the treatment he needed before releasing it back into the jungle.

We do the same with our thoughts and feelings. We ignore them, fight them, pull them and push them. Then we're trapped. We don't realise that if we let go of trying to fix them, we'd feel free of their grip.

JOKE

My book on 'Letting Go' was a flop.
Apparently, it was too gripping.

3.

Getting Flexible

ACT can be as simple or as complex as you wish it to be. At its simplest, ACT is about living a meaningful life. How? By focusing on improving just one thing – your psychological flexibility.

Psychological flexibility is your ability to flexibly and fluidly move towards what's most important for you in your life, while skilfully managing your inner experiences.

Another way of understanding this is to consider all the actions you take in your life. You're always doing something – even if it's just sitting down and snoozing.

You can think of actions as helpful if they move you towards what's meaningful in your life and unhelpful if they move you away from living a meaningful life.

For example, maybe you love learning and teaching. So, you decide to make a difference by becoming a teacher. A helpful action would be to go for an interview. Helpful actions can bring up tricky feelings that you may have been avoiding.

Unhelpful actions could include using strategies to avoid difficult thoughts and feelings, such as excessive drinking to avoid feeling sad, taking drugs to avoid boredom or procrastinating by watching TV instead of applying for fulfilling jobs.

ACT encourages you to explore if your actions are the right choice for you right now, or not. Sometimes they can be – for example, you may need to take a break or give yourself a treat. And if not, the ACT exercises in Part 2 and Part 3 will help you to take more helpful actions towards living a life of greater purpose and fulfilment, and use your flexibility skills to manage the difficult thoughts and feelings that come up along the way.

JOKE

How Flexible Are You?
I was at the gym the other day and asked the personal trainer if they could teach me to do the splits.
'How flexible are you?', she asked.
I said, 'Well, I can do most days apart from Mondays and Fridays.'

METAPHOR

The Noisy Park Bench

Imagine you're sitting on a bench in your favourite park. The sun is shining, the birds are singing, and you're just watching the world go by. Then, out of nowhere, someone sits next to you. They're loud, they criticise you, judge you and keep going on and on. This person is like one of those annoying worries that pops into your head when you're trying to get on with life.

So, you tell them to just shut up, but they won't. You put on headphones to distract you and drown out the noise, but then you can't enjoy the park. You try pushing them off the bench, but they just push back even harder. You end up spending all your time, effort and energy trying all sorts of elaborate tricks to get rid of them, but again and again, the noise and criticism comes back.

So you try something radically different. Instead of trying to get the noise to stop, you just decide to let them be. You don't listen to their conversation; you don't let it bother you. You just refocus your attention on enjoying the breeze, the sunshine on your face, and the laughter of kids playing around.

This person talking next to you is just noise. You can hear it, but you don't have to listen to it or let it ruin your time in the park. Just like when you're worried or upset, you don't have to let those feelings take over. You can know they're there, but still enjoy the good things and have a nice day.

ACT teaches you the skills to make peace with your inner noise and refocus your attention on what matters, one tiny step at a time. And sometimes, because you're so focused on what's important, meaningful or fun, you forget about the noise altogether. But even if you do notice the noise, that's fine. You make space for all experiences, both the noise as well as the bird song and green grass.

4.

The Problem with
Problem-Solving

Your brain is designed to solve problems. Baby's crying? You try feeding him. Website not working? Contact a specialist to fix it. Humans can't help but find problems and then try to fix them. That's how we roll.

But this same urge to fix things through thinking can play havoc when turned inwards. Feeling anxious? Okay, I'll avoid that feeling and do some relaxation. Thinking negatively? Okay, I'll block my negative thoughts and think more positive ones.

This approach is totally understandable and normal. It's the way your brain is wired – to fix all the problems you meet. However, ACT researchers have realised that this idea of fixing your feelings and thoughts is at the root of much human suffering.

Here's the issue. If you don't want to think a thought (such as 'I'm not good enough'), it'll just get stronger –

because you're inadvertently giving it more attention. You're actively making an effort to avoid it.

And if you think a certain feeling is bad and to be avoided, like sadness, you may begin to fear it, which makes the feeling stronger. You start to feel sad about feeling sad. Or anxious about feeling anxious. Or even angry about feeling angry. Without realising it, you amplify the original feeling or thought.

Trying to get rid of your tricky thoughts and feelings isn't the solution. In fact, the act of trying to get rid of them becomes the problem itself!

Hundreds of studies have found avoidance to be the root cause of all sorts of mental health challenges, leading to a decreased quality of life.

You can summarise this insight as follows:

'What you avoid, you invite. What you accept, you transform.'

JOKE

> **Twice Is Better**
> I saw a documentary called How to Reduce Your Life's Problems by 50%. Naturally, I watched it twice.

STORY Stuck in the Mud

I was once visiting a small palace in India that was surrounded by mud. It was very quiet, which surprised me, but it didn't stop me going there. I confidently walked towards the palace in the mud. I noticed there was a thin stream of water on my path, and then more mud.

'No big deal,' I thought, and I jumped over the stream of water. Bad idea! I immediately sunk into the mud on the other side. Both my legs were stuck deep in the mud!

I tried to struggle my way out, but it didn't work. I was stuck, and the more I struggled, the more I felt stuck in the mud. I started to feel scared. 'What if I never get out? What if I keep sinking deeper?' I thought. I could easily have ended up panicking as I frantically tried harder and harder to get out.

Fortunately, I decided to try something different. I stopped struggling. Struggling wasn't working. Then, when I stopped the struggle, I was able to have an idea. I realised I needed to slip my feet out of my shoes to free myself. From there, I needed to open up my body, lie down and gently roll out of the mud.

It worked! I was free. Funnily enough, a few minutes later, a kid managed to get my shoes out of the mud and sold them back to me! True story!

If you're struggling with your thoughts or feelings and you're finding yourself sinking deeper, recall this story. The struggling wasn't the solution – it was the problem.

5.

Reducing Suffering

Good news – ACT is designed to help reduce your suffering.

In ACT, we distinguish between pain and suffering. Pain is inevitable. You're bound to experience challenges that are painful. But suffering is optional. Here's a formula:

Pain x Avoidance = Suffering

Everyone experiences pain. You're bound to experience some physical pain and perhaps even chronic pain. But beyond physical pain is the mental pain of difficult thoughts and feelings. Feelings of sadness, despair and loneliness. Memories of past hurts and worries about future uncertainties.

Suffering is different. Suffering is something you may be creating, quite often unconsciously, by trying to run away, fight with or deny pain. It's this habitual reaction to your pain that generates suffering.

For example, if you feel sad and you make lots of effort to deny, suppress or avoid feeling sad, this leads to an unnecessary deepening of your sadness – and that's suffering.

ACT teaches you flexibility skills so you don't compound your pain. With ACT, you'll learn to make space for your feelings, just like the sky makes space for all sorts of weather. The sky can make space for dark clouds, wind, rain, storms, thunder and lightning. So you too can develop your ability to make space for the internal storms that come and go.

By learning to apply the skills of ACT, you're able to reduce your suffering and increase your sense of fulfilment in life. You achieve this by learning to both accept and step back from painful experiences, and to motivate yourself through taking meaningful action.

METAPHOR   The Lost Keys and the Lost Temper

Imagine one day you lose your keys. That's the first problem. It happens sometimes, and it's not something you planned. Now, you have two choices. You can either get really upset, start yelling, and throw things around looking for them. That's like adding a second problem on top of the first one. You're not just missing your keys now, but you're also feeling angry and making a mess.

Or you could take a deep breath, think about where you last saw your keys, and start looking calmly. Maybe you ask someone for help or use a spare key. This way, you're dealing with the first problem – the lost keys – without creating a new one.

The point is, sometimes things go wrong, like losing your keys. That's the pain, and it's often out of your control. But getting really upset or angry about it? That's like adding a second problem, the suffering that you can have some control over, with practice. The idea is to handle the pain without causing yourself suffering.

This suffering, the lost temper, is an experience you can do something about. Using the flexibility skills you learn in ACT (see Part 2 of this book), you'll be better able to see the thoughts as more like what they are: sounds and pictures in your head. And you can begin to make peace with your feelings too – by just letting them be. In this way, you suffer less and focus more on what really matters in your life.

JOKE

Keyrings
What's the main reason for a keyring?
So you can lose all your keys in one go.

6.

Focus on Helpful Thoughts, Not Absolute Truths

In practising ACT, you'll realise that there's a whole stream of thoughts in your head. Some of them may be true, but many of them are not.

For example, you may think, 'I'm never gonna understand this ACT stuff.' Is that true? Well, that's hard to say.

You may also think, 'I'm going to get sick.' That thought is true. We all get ill at some point. But does that mean you should keep thinking that all the time? If you do, you won't be able to focus on your life.

It's much better to think of some of your thoughts as helpful and others as unhelpful. Helpful thoughts are thoughts that will move you towards a life of meaning and vitality. Unhelpful thoughts move you away from a meaningful and vital life.

You may have had terrible experiences in the past, but you can't wipe that away. There's no way to press delete so all your past memories disappear. But you can decide which thoughts will be more helpful to move you towards a rich and meaningful life. ACT encourages you to use the helpful thoughts and let the unhelpful thoughts, even if they're true, just float on by.

This is good news. It means you don't have to consider whether the harsh, critical and judgemental thoughts popping into your head are true or not – thoughts like, 'I'm useless,' 'I will never be happy' or 'I'm unlovable.' Simply engage with these thoughts if they are helpful. And if they're not, use the flexibility skills you'll learn in this book to allow the other thoughts to move on. You don't need to fix anything.

JOKE

> **I'm Telling the Truth!**
> What do you get if you ask a politician to say 'the truth, the whole truth, and nothing but the truth'?
> Three different answers!

The Young Child

If you're talking to a three-year-old child, would you teach her what's helpful or what's true?

If you want to teach her what's true, you could open up the newspaper and show her all the worst things happening in the world. You could tell her that you and your whole family will one day all die. You might tell her that all the fairy tales are untrue, or tell her all about her inadequacies.

I hope you don't! Because although these things may all be true, they're not helpful facts to share with a very young child. It's far more helpful to share things that will support their development. This may include some of the sad things happening in the world, but you can share them in a way that leads to their growth, understanding and resilience.

In the same way, consider the thoughts you find helpful for creating a fulfilling life for you and your loved ones.

7.

When is ACT Beneficial?

ACT can't help everyone with everything – no one therapy or training approach can. But the research so far shows it's helped many people with challenges like anxiety, depression, psychosis, chronic pain and panic. ACT has also been found to help children learn better, help businesses thrive, help athletes excel and help therapists become more resilient.

Why does it seem to help with such a diverse range of problems? The answer – because in theory, and according to the research, ACT should work wherever the human mind goes. And the human mind goes in many different areas!

ACT is called a 'trans-diagnostic' approach, meaning it focuses on core processes that may cause issues for humans, and it helps people to overcome those issues. In other words, ACT has the potential to be helpful, no matter what your challenges you face.

This is useful to know, because if you find ACT helps with a particular challenge in your life, you may want to continue using the skills you've learnt to prepare for future challenges too. In this way, you can continue to reap the benefits.

Having said this, people seem to find ACT particularly beneficial when they're feeling stuck. That's because ACT takes you away from trying to fix your thoughts and feelings and towards kindly making inner space for them. It also teaches you practical ways to find meaning in your life. And maybe this radically different approach is what's right for you, too.

Can You Cycle?

If you've learnt to cycle, you know that you're not just able to ride the bike you learnt on – you can ride pretty much any standard bicycle.

Almost every bike has handlebars. It has brakes and gears you know how to use. And it has lights, a seat, wheels, and so on.

Once you've learnt the core skills of cycling, you can ride pretty much anywhere in the world on almost any bike. You've got the skills!

However, that doesn't make you the best cyclist in the world. The more you practise, train and get feedback, the better you get. If you just cycle without awareness, that's dangerous. You need to stay awake, open and engaged – and cycle in the right direction.

In the same way, once you've learnt and practised the six core flexibility skills of ACT, you can learn to apply ACT to every area of your life – ACT can work wherever your mind goes.

> **JOKE**
>
> **We're On a Roll!**
> Why could the bike not stand up on its own?
> It was two tyred.

Part 2

Applying ACT

In this part, you'll get to the heart of the ACT model. You'll learn what the six flexibility skills are and how to nurture and grow these skills in your life. And you'll begin to explore how these six skills connect with each other.

If you like getting practical, you'll love this part as it's full of useful exercises to help develop your flexibility skills and get your life moving forwards in meaningful ways.

8.

The Six Flexibility Skills

ACT was developed in the lab. After many thousands of studies, amazingly the researchers discovered just six core skills that were central to a flourishing, resilient life – no matter who you are.

To help you remember these six core flexibility skills, I've put them in order to spell the word **ACTION**:

A – Acceptance
C – Cognitive Defusion
T – Transcendent Self
I – In the Present Moment
O – Open Up to Your Values
N – Navigate with Meaningful Action

They also fit neatly on a hexagon (see the psychological flexibility ACTION diagram below), which gives a simple visual way of summarising the model.

Acceptance

Navigate with
Meaningful
Action

Cognitive Defusion

**Psychological
Flexibility**

Open Up to
Your Values

Transcendent Self

In the Moment

As you read this part of the book, see if you can memorise these six skills, using the word 'ACTION' to help you. You could write them on a small card and carry it with you. In the next six chapters, I explain each of these skills, one at a time, together with a practical exercise to help you use and develop each skill.

STORY The Night I Got Stuck in the Snow

I was driving in London late at night, and it began to snow lightly. I thought I'd be okay but, as the journey continued, the snow got heavier and heavier. My car started to skid a little, so I drove slowly. As I turned off a major road, I had to drive up a small hill. My car got stuck.

I couldn't move. I tried to accelerate out of the snow, but the wheels just couldn't get any grip.

After lots of wheel spinning, I tried a different tactic. I tried accelerating very slowly. That didn't work. I got out and dug some snow out from under the tyre. But that didn't work either. I tried bouncing on the back of the car, but still no luck. Then I asked for some help. The people tried pushing the car as I revved the engine. Still no luck. Finally, one person bounced the car up and down, the other pushed the car and I accelerated. Then I finally managed to get out!

I had to take six different actions to get unstuck, in different combinations. In the same way, whenever you feel stuck, overwhelmed or hopeless, move around the six flexibility skills. Don't get fixed on just developing any one skill – they work best when you're flexible in your application of them.

JOKE

| **A Cool Joke** |
| What did the icy road say to the car? |
| 'Want to go for a spin?' |

9.

Flexibility Skill: Acceptance

Acceptance is a tricky word. In ACT, acceptance does *not* mean:

- Resignation
- Tolerance
- Putting up with things
- Liking or wanting an experience

So, what does acceptance mean? Think of how you may use the word acceptance when giving someone a gift. When you give a lovely gift to a friend, you might say 'Will you accept this?'

This is the spirit of acceptance we mean when we're talking about accepting your feelings.

Why accept these difficult inner experiences? Because when you do the opposite of acceptance – avoidance – you're likely setting yourself up to fail. The experience will come back stronger as you're seeing the experience as negative and giving it more attention, perhaps unconsciously. In ACT, it's often said: 'If you don't want it, you got it!'

Many people don't like or understand what acceptance means in ACT. So here's some other words that may work better for you and may make more sense. Imagine you're struggling with anxiety. You could say you are:

- *Making room* for anxiety
- *Making space* for anxiety
- *Expanding* to allow anxiety to be present
- *Allowing* anxiety to be present
- Letting anxiety to just be
- *Creating inner space* for anxiety to arise

Your feelings are not problems to be fixed; they are experiences to be honoured. When you open your heart to your internal experiences, you're able to create the inner space necessary for cultivating acceptance. The following story helps to illustrate this.

METAPHOR **Talking To Your Shadow**

Imagine your difficult emotions — whether they're sadness, worry, panic, guilt, or revulsion — as a dark shadow on your favourite walking path. It's natural you might have tried to dodge or outrun this shadow for a long time. But these tactics seem to be failing; the shadow always reappears. You're weary of sidestepping, sprinting, and hiding from it, and you're prepared for a new approach.

Instead of skirting around the shadow, consider doing the opposite of your usual response. This will feel very strange to you, but you've had enough. You're ready to try something new, as all other approaches haven't seemed to work.

Picture yourself walking straight into your shadow. Even though it's intimidating, you resolve to face it head-on, curious about what will happen if you stop avoiding it.

You continue your walk towards your shadow, acknowledging its cool presence without fear. You understand it's just a shadow — it can't hurt you. You might even start talking to it, saying, "Why do you follow me, sadness?" or "What do you need, anxiety?" Instead of shooing it away, you listen to what it might be trying to tell you.

Take a moment to really hear the whisper of your shadow. When you've heard enough, you metaphorically embrace it. This is the essence of acceptance: allowing the shadow to merge with your path, realising it's a part of you, and maybe even discovering the valuable lessons it has to offer.

After all, a shadow only exists because you are present in the light.

ACT Exercise – Acceptance

To develop your acceptance skills, try this:

1. Take a few slow, conscious breaths and gently close your eyes (or you can keep your eyes open if you prefer).

2. When you're ready, bring to mind a difficulty you're going through that you're willing to work with. A difficulty you feel ready to explore.

3. Bring the challenges associated with the experience to mind. It will feel somewhat uncomfortable, which is needed for this exercise.

4. Now, see if you can be 100% willing to feel the feelings associated with the experience for however long you choose. Perhaps a minute or two. Or maybe just a few seconds. Whatever you decide, choose to commit to welcoming the experience fully, just as it is. Being accepting is a choice, not a feeling.

5. Reflect on these statements slowly to give you a sense of how to be with the feeling:

   - Hold the feeling like you'd hold a delicate flower.

   - See the feeling as you'd see a beautiful sunset.

   - Care for the experience as you'd care for an upset young baby.

6. Complete the exercise with a few slow, deep breaths to finish.

10.

Flexibility Skill: Cognitive Defusion

You've probably had that experience when you get lost in your thoughts, and your mind starts going to all the things that could go wrong in your life. You might start to think 'What if I lose my job?' or 'I just can't get on with my partner' or any number of other such thoughts. This may last a few minutes or more. By the time you snap out of this way of thinking, you may feel more anxious or depressed – as if you've taken a train and got off at a stop that you didn't really want to get off at.

This process of getting lost in your thoughts – and taking these thoughts to be facts – is called cognitive *fusion*. Why fusion? When two things are fused, they are stuck together – and that's what happens to your thoughts when they stay with you like this. You get stuck to your thoughts and believe them to be completely true in that moment.

Sometimes it's fine to get lost in your thoughts – like when you're reading a book, watching a movie or daydreaming of nice places you could go. Fusion is no problem at all at such times.

But when you are fused to your thoughts and they are unhelpful, that's when fusion becomes an issue: when your thoughts stop you from doing what matters to you. Being fused to unhelpful thoughts allows them to push you around and may mean you choose to avoid the very activities that make your life so enjoyable, rich and meaningful.

In ACT, the opposite of fusion is *defusion* (or *cognitive defusion*). Defusion is the skill of seeing thoughts for what they are – just sounds or images in your head – so your unhelpful thoughts don't have as much of an impact on you.

The good news is you can develop the skill of defusing from unhelpful thoughts. Meditation was once thought to be the only way to achieve this skill of stepping back from your thoughts. But ACT has discovered hundreds of ways, some of them very unusual, and I share a few in the next section. All you need to do is try them out and see which ones work best for you.

ACT Exercises – Cognitive Defusion

Try these techniques to unhook you from your unhelpful thoughts:

- **Disobey your mind on purpose.** Normally, when we're fused to our thoughts, we just automatically do what our minds tell us. This is a simple, unusual and powerful technique to show you that it's possible for your mind to say one thing and for you to do another. For example, keep saying in your mind 'I can't walk, I can't walk' as you walk around the room. Or keep saying in your head 'I can't move my eyes, I can't move my eyes' while you move your eyes around. It's easy and fun to try!

- **Notice you're having a thought.** Start with an unhelpful thought you have, like 'I'm such a bad mother/father' or whatever your thought is. Take your time to really connect with that thought and notice the discomfort you feel. Then, say in your mind: 'I notice I'm having the thought "XXXX."' Say it again. Consider whether doing this helps to distance you from the thought.

- **Sing to a tune.** Defusion works by helping you realise your thoughts are just words – sounds in your head. One powerful way to achieve this is by singing the words to a tune. You can use any tune. Try singing your unhelpful thought to a familiar tune like 'Happy Birthday'. For example, imagine singing the thought 'I'm very bad' to the tune of 'Happy Birthday'. You can do this in your head, or sing it out loud if you want to confuse anyone nearby!

- **Give your mind a name.** By giving your mind a name, you help to create some separation between you and your mind – so you can relate to your mind instead of your mind controlling you. You can call your mind George, for example. Or just call it Mind! Then when it rebels, simply say, 'Thanks for sharing, George.' Or simply, 'Thanks, Mind.'

- **Write on a card.** If you have a thought that is unhelpful and yet is having an impact on your life, try writing it down on a piece of card and carrying it around with you throughout the day. Every now and then, pull the card out and read it. This shows you that your thought is just a sentence, a bunch of words, and you don't need to eliminate those words to move on with your life; you can carry them around with you *and* get on with your life. It's simple, yet effective for some.

Keep practising the defusion exercises several times a day and also whenever you notice you've become fused with unhelpful thoughts.

Watching Bubbles Float By

METAPHOR This is both a metaphor and a visualisation you can try to help you defuse from your thoughts. Read the rest of this passage, and then spend a few minutes doing the visualisation.

Imagine you're sitting in a park. Some children are blowing bubbles some distance away. These bubbles keep floating past you gently in the wind.

You watch as each bubble enters your view and floats past, one after the other.

Each time a thought pops into your head, image placing the thought inside the bubble. The thought can have the form of a word, a sentence or an image. All you need to do is place the thought inside each bubble as it floats by.

Each time you do this, you create a distance between you and your thoughts. You become less fused to your thoughts. It doesn't matter if you have lots of thoughts, or very few. Just keep placing them in the bubbles. You can even put your thoughts about this exercise inside the bubbles!

Try this visualisation for a minute or two every day to develop your flexibility skill of cognitive defusion.

JOKE

> **Blowing Bubbles**
> Why did the ACT teacher share so many jokes in sessions?
> 'They wanted to be 'pop-ular''

11.

Flexibility Skill:
Transcendent Self

Have you ever considered the question: 'Who, exactly, am I?' Are you simply your name? Well, surely you'd be the same person with a different name, so that can't be who you are. Perhaps you think of yourself as your body. But even if you lost your arms or legs, you'd still be the same person. Okay, perhaps you think of yourself as your mind and brain, with your thoughts and feelings and memories. But your inner experiences are changing almost every moment, so how can that be you? If you change your mind about something, are you a different person? And are you constantly changing?

You may have a sense of having been the same person ever since you were little, and yet your body has changed so much, as have your thoughts and feelings.

That 'sense of self', which seems to have remained the same since you were very young, can be considered your true self. Here in the West, there's no common term we use to describe this fundamental part of our being. You could call it your *transcendent self*. Or there are many other names you could give it, such as your:

- Observing self
- Witnessing self
- Awareness self
- Enduring self
- Conscious self

Call it whatever you wish! It is beyond names, because it is not a 'thing' as such. It's the part that observes everything else. It's the observer.

Why is tuning into your transcendent self skill important? Because it can give you a sense of inner space, freedom and peace. Without that sense of being an observer of your thoughts and feelings, it's easy to get caught up and ordered around by them. By stepping back and being the observer of your thoughts and feelings, in some sense you are free of them. Thoughts and feelings are then a part of you, but not all of you – you're bigger than any one experience.

As the observing self, you can't be touched by your difficult thoughts and feelings. They come and go as they wish. You're like a giant container that holds all thoughts, feelings and any other conscious experience you have.

Personally, I like to think of my observing self as pure, perfect and complete. A core part of my being that doesn't need improving or fixing in any way. Already whole and free. The source of peace and love. A sanctuary I can return to at any time. And a part of me that connects me deeply with others.

Don't feel you have to consider your transcendent self in this way. View your transcendent self in a way that is meaningful to you. If you're not sure, that's perfectly normal. As you practice these ACT skills, you will begin to create your own personal relationship with your transcendent self.

ACT Exercise – Transcendent Self

Try this short reflection. Say each statement slowly and reflect on it before moving on to the next.

1. Begin by sitting comfortably and taking three deep, slow breaths. You can have your eyes open or closed.

2. Notice your physical body. Then say to yourself: 'I am the observer of my body, and so I'm not my body.'

3. Notice any thoughts popping into your head. Then say to yourself: 'I'm the observer of my thoughts, so I'm not my thoughts.'

4. Become aware of how you're feeling right now. Then say: 'I'm the observer of my feelings, and so I'm not my feelings.'

5. Take three more deep, slow breaths

6. Say to yourself: 'I am the observer of all experiences. I am much bigger than any thoughts or feelings. As the transcendent self, I am completely peaceful/compassionate/silent/free/at one [use whichever words work for you].'

7. Finish with three deep, slow breaths.

8. Open your eyes (if they've been closed) and return your focus to whatever meaningful activity you want to do next.

Try this exercise a few times and notice the effect it has. You could also try the exercise when you're overwhelmed with painful thoughts or feelings. The exercise can help you step back and view these experiences from a wider perspective.

METAPHOR The Mirror and Its Reflections

Imagine for a moment that your awareness is a large mirror, standing tall in a quiet room. This mirror has been here forever, its surface smooth and unblemished. It doesn't judge; it simply reflects everything that stands before it — every colour, every shape, every movement.

Now picture every thought and feeling that stirs within you is like a person stepping in front of this mirror. Some of them smile brightly, bringing thoughts of joy and laughter, their happiness reflected for a moment before they step away. Others might frown, their reflections full of worries, doubts, or sadness, casting a temporary shadow over the mirror's surface.

But the important thing to remember is that the mirror, your awareness, remains unchanged. It doesn't cling to the smiles or try to push away the frowns. It doesn't hold onto the reflections of yesterday or reach out for those of tomorrow. It simply is. It reflects the here and now.

Learning to view your thoughts and feelings as mere reflections means you don't have to react to each one. Instead, you can observe them with a gentle curiosity, understanding that they are not you; they are simply passing through the vast, open space of your awareness, like reflections in a mirror.

12.s

Flexibility Skill:
In the Present Moment

In one famous Harvard study, researchers wanted to find out how often people's minds are not in the present moment. Any guesses? Amazingly, people's minds were wandering and not present for 47% of the time. That's almost half of their lives!

Imagine if you didn't have the ability to stay focused on the present moment at all. Your mind would be totally lost in the world of the past and future, and you wouldn't be able to do simple things like have a conversation with a friend or read this book. We've all had the experience of having scattered attention. The good news is that the skill of *being present* can be developed – as many studies have shown. And it doesn't need to take too long, either.

You can be present in only two areas – your inner world of thoughts and feelings, and the outer world around you, through your senses.

There are great benefits to being able to be present and move your attention from one focus to another as and when you need to. For example, recently I went out for a walk in nature. But my mind was caught up in thinking about work. By using my skill of being present, I was able to notice when my mind wandered and refocus on the beautiful trees, grass, flowers, sky, clouds and birds. I felt refreshed and recharged. Without the skill of being present, I would easily have been lost in thoughts about work and missed the beauty around me. It would have been like a walk in the office instead of in the park.

STORY Being present is also hugely beneficial when faced with challenges. Let me share another example. Recently, I received an aggressive and rude text message. It was out of the blue. I felt hurt and angry. My mind began dwelling on all the reasons why this person sent that rude message: I was thinking thoughts like 'Why is she so rude?', judging her and considering the many ways I could respond, as well as feeling frustrated by the situation.

I noticed where my mind was going. I knew responding out of anger wouldn't be helpful. So, I decided to be more centred and present before I responded. I used my skill of being present as best I could. Each time I noticed my mind wandering to the text, I refocused my attention back to the feeling of my body, a present-moment experience.

That night, as I lay in bed, I kept refocusing my mind, kindly and gently, back to my body and breathing. And I had a surprisingly good night's sleep. Without the skill of being in the present moment, I probably wouldn't have slept much at all. One text could have upset a night's sleep and therefore affected the next day too.

The echo of that experience stayed with me for a while. But by being present, I was able to move forward in my life and let go of what I can't control, which is other people's messages to me. When I called back, I discovered that she wrote that message because of her own issues and anger, and the situation was resolved sooner than I thought.

As you can see in the examples, the flexibility skill of being present is invaluable in leading a richer, more meaningful life. It can both enhance pleasant experiences and help you to skilfully navigate challenging situations. It can also enhance your normal, everyday activities like making a cup of tea or coffee, or even breathing.

Being present isn't always easy as you probably know. The mind loves worrying. But I've found even a 1% improvement in being present makes a difference in a day. Taking just one extra second before you send that text back. Taking one deep breath before you complain to your partner. Spending one moment noticing the colour of the sky on your walk. All these small moments create ripples of peace, that gently create a more joyful life.

ACT Exercise – In the Present Moment

There are many ways to develop the flexibility skill of being present. You can do it in your everyday life by simply paying attention to whatever you're doing, when you're doing it. Mundane or routine tasks like ironing or showering can give you great opportunities to cultivate present-moment awareness.

Present-moment awareness can be developed through connecting with your senses. Your senses are always in the present. By focusing on your senses, your attention is less likely to be caught up in replaying events from the past or worrying about the future. The skill of presence is a gateway and a supporter of all the other flexibility skills.

Here's a simple way to begin developing flexible present-moment awareness that takes a few minutes at most.

1. Start by taking three slow, deep breaths. Feel the actual sensation of each breath.

2. Notice five different things around you that you can see. Be aware of their colours and any shadows around them.

3. Notice four different sensations in your body. Be curious.

4. Notice three different sounds you can hear. They can be sounds that are close or in the distance.

5. Notice two things you can taste in your mouth (tricky!). You might be able to taste your most recent meal, perhaps.

6. Notice one thing you can smell.

7. Now finish by taking three slow, full breaths once again. Really feel and be present with each breath if you can.

8. Re-engage with whatever you need to do next with this present-moment awareness as best you can.

STORY Taking the Dog for a Walk

Imagine you have a dog and you're taking it for a walk in your local park. You've had a lot on your mind, and as you walk your dog, your mind is lost in thoughts.

You're worried about what your boss will say to you tomorrow after reading an email from them. Your worries go on and on. You think: 'Why does your boss want to talk to you?' What if you get fired? Why didn't you get that last sale closed last week?'

And then, you notice you have a message on your phone. You open the message and it says your boss wasn't upset with you about your sales figures – they'd sent the email to the wrong person!

Suddenly, you realise that while you were lost in thought, worrying about something that wasn't even true, you'd missed a beautiful sunset. But your dog, who doesn't have email or a job, seemed to be fully present and enjoying the sounds and smells in the park very much.

Next time you go for a walk, set the gentle intention to be more present to your surroundings, so you can enjoy each walk just as much as a dog would. Even just a moment or two of presence counts.

JOKE

It's a Sign
What did the sign outside the mindfulness retreat centre say?
'Inquire within.'

13.

Flexibility Skill: Open Up to Your Heart's Values

Values are at the heart of ACT. All the flexibility skills we have looked at so far are designed to help you manage your thoughts and feelings so you are able to live in alignment with your values.

'What are values?' you may ask. Your *values* are ongoing qualities that embody how you wish to live your life. Ongoing because you can apply them in every moment.

Some examples of values include living kindly, curiously, openly, courageously, mindfully, creatively, playfully, fairly, compassionately, caringly, wisely, and so on. There are hundreds of them. Notice they are words ending in - ly. This is because values are adverbs - something you can do – not just ideas or concepts.

Values are NOT goals. Why? Because values can't be reached. Values are like a direction – like travelling west. You might travel west every day, but you never get there! It's a direction. In the same way, if you value curiosity, you don't finish being curious! Every day is a chance to be curious and learn something new.

Why are values so important? Because if you don't know what your values are, you're a bit like a ship lost at sea. You don't have a sense of direction. You can end up drifting aimlessly for weeks, months and years. And even if you achieve your goals, they can feel empty of fulfilment.

Once you're clear on what your values are, you have purpose. You have direction. And you can channel your energies in that direction. Every time you move forward in that directly, no matter how small, you are likely to feel more fulfilled and energised.

The great thing about values is you don't need any time to reach them. You can connect with your values right now. For example, why are you reading this book? Is it because you like learning, discovering new things, trying something new or engaging in personal growth? Any of these could be one of your values. If you think about why you are reading these words, you may feel a bit more engaged and purposeful because you're doing something that's meaningful to you.

Your values don't change much. They might shift and change throughout your life, but they rarely change by much. They give you a sense of what you stand for in your life. My values include doing things kindly, curiously, creatively and playfully. They've not changed for many years.

By getting to know your values and acting on one or more of them daily, you'll be able to live a more meaningful life. And this will give you a sense of fulfilment and motivation to help you through life's challenges.

Remember, your values are yours. You choose them for yourself. They reflect what you *want* to do and the kind of person you *want* to be, not what you *should* want to do or the kind of person you *should* want to be. They come from your heart. They are qualities you are naturally drawn to that end up being a powerful source of inner motivation and purpose.

ACT Exercise – Discovering Your Values

There are several ways to discover what your values are. Here's three different approaches you could try.

1. **Attending your 80th.** Imagine you're able to attend your own 80th (or 90th or 100th!) birthday party. Take your time to visualise the whole experience. Who would you want to be there? What would you want them to say about you? What qualities would you wish them to say you have? Listen carefully to them. The qualities you wish them to share about you can give you an idea of the kind of values that are important to you.

2. **Considering your heroes.** Consider three people you really look up to in life. People who may or may not be famous. Maybe they are family members, past or present. Maybe leaders in society. Perhaps an old friend or teacher. Once you come up with your three, reflect – what is it about them that you really respect? What qualities do they have that you wish to cultivate in yourself? These could be your values.

3. **Flipping your pain.** This approach is surprisingly powerful. Consider what you find painful in life. What upsets you? What makes you feel uncomfortable or distressed? It may turn out that the other side of this pain is one of your values. For example, if you suffer from social anxiety, it's likely because one of your values is

connecting with others. And it may be causing you anxiety because it matters to you so much.

Remember, you don't need to decide what your values are today and stick with them for the rest of your life. Take time to explore your values. There are many values – experiment with applying a value for a few weeks and see how it feels for you. By experimenting with a value, you can try it out. If it feels fulfilling to engage with that value, you could be onto a winner. If the value doesn't seem to resonate, perhaps try another one for size.

METAPHOR Living Your Values

Imagine two people who are keen to be promoted at work. One of them is more value-focused, called Val. The other one is more goal-focused, called Go.

Val knows her values are learning, courage and kindness. So when the chance for promotion comes up, Val decides to apply for it because although she's nervous about the extra responsibility, she knows she'll learn lots of new things in the role. She sets her goal, based on her values. And she uses her flexibility skills to manage the difficult thoughts and feelings that inevitably come up.

Go also notices the chance for promotion, and she's determined to get it. But there are no clear values behind her goal. She does everything she can to get the promotion. She does extra favours for her boss, and she lies about her co-workers (saying they're not pulling their weight, and so on). She hates her current role and believes she will only be happy once she gets the promotion. That's her goal.

Unfortunately, someone else gets the promotion. Not Val or Go. Val is a bit disappointed, but she congratulates the new person and even gets them a gift, satisfying her value of kindness. Go is furious and quits, leaving her frustrated and not having another job to go to.

Pursuing meaningful values is fulfilling and an enjoyable life-long journey. When you are focused on your values, you can of course enjoy the success and happiness in achieving any one goal. But you know it's simply a step along the journey. Pursing a goal without values can lead to a brief high when you're successful, but it may be followed by a sense of emptiness. Happiness or peace is short-lived in the absence of value-based living.

14.

Flexibility Skill: Navigate with Meaningful Action

Taking action and cultivating habits in line with your values is an important step in ACT. 'Navigating' applies to this skill because you can set goals and choose actions that align with your values.

Values are not 'good' and goals are not 'bad'. Values tell you which direction to go and value-based goals help you *take meaningful action* in that direction. You can set small, easy, meaningful goals as well as more bold, ambitious, long-term goals. The purpose of the goals is to move you towards a life that you're excited about.

Creating a meaningful life is not usually easy. You will meet challenges – and the biggest challenge will probably be managing the voice and the images between your ears. The good news is you can keep using the other flexibility skills to make space for the thoughts and feelings that'll keep coming up, without getting overwhelmed by them.

When setting your goals, take a **SMARTER** approach, which may seem a familiar concept – but I've adapted this to make it ACT friendly:

S = Specific – Aim to take a particular action, not a vague one.

M = Meaningful – Link your goals to one or more of your values.

A = Achievable – Keep most of your goals small and easily achievable.

R = Rewarding – Remember, some self-praise can help!

T = Time-based – Consider when exactly you will do this.

E = Expand– Make space for thoughts and feelings to come and go.

R = Reflect – Ask yourself, 'What did I learn? What worked and what didn't?'

So, for example, if you're really not enjoying your job and would love to get a new one, then this is a SMARTER way to do it:

S – Set a **specific** goal, like spending 15 minutes a day searching for a new job.

M – Ensure your new job is **meaningful** and aligned with your values. If you value creativity, search for a job that allows space for you to be creative.

A – Be realistic in what you'll **achieve.** You probably won't get the first job you apply for. Start with a small goal to apply for one job this week.

R – Celebrate with a smile or a punch in the air as a little **reward** when you apply for a new job! Every application is a step closer towards your dream.

T – Remember not to be vague. Exactly what **time** every day will you do this job research? And on what day will you be sending that first CV?

E – **Expand** and open up. Use exercises from the first four flexibility skills (acceptance, cognitive defusion, transcendent self and in the moment) to make space for your self-limiting thoughts and challenging feelings to come and go. Those thoughts and feelings are perfectly normal to have when you're moving towards meaningful goals.

R – **Reflect** on how it's going. What have you learnt so far? Did the action feel meaningful? Did you do the action? If not, make the goal smaller or change the goal – there's no need to give up or beat yourself up. Taking meaning action is a learning process, and reflection is a key part of that process. Other questions to consider include: Who could support you in this goal? What other ways could you try? What would make it easier? How can you take a more creative or playful approach? You could even write your answers down in a diary or journal.

STORY   But What If I Fail?

Recently, I wanted to offer a new kind of workshop. But I was nervous about it. My mind started saying, 'I'm not sure if people will like this content. What if I get confused and don't teach it well? What will they say? What would they think of me if I got so nervous that I couldn't explain it properly? And I'm someone who's supposed to be mindful?! That would look terrible!'

I reflected on what values were linked to this. The workshop was in line with my values of helping others, and learning and teaching. It also linked to my value of being courageous and connecting with others.

So I broke the goal down into little steps using the SMARTER approach: writing the description, setting a date, advertising the workshop, and so on. Then I started working through the list, step by step, remembering my values and practising acceptance, openness and presence. I reflected whenever I didn't complete any of my mini-goals along the way.

Some actions brought up feelings of anxiety and scary thoughts. But I did the workshop anyway, using the ACT flexibility skills to make space for my anxious thoughts rather than trying to get rid of them. I'm grateful for my ACT skills, which supported my journey – otherwise, I may have not done the workshop at all if I'd started thinking that the anxiety was a sign that I should avoid the challenge.

ACT Exercise – Setting SMARTER Goals That Are Exciting, Effective and Meaningful

When it comes to setting meaningful goals in ACT, where do you start? Begin by deciding which *domain* of your life you wish to focus on.

Here are four common domains of life you might consider:

- Work and education
- Leisure
- Health and wellbeing
- Relationships – personal, friends and family

Follow these steps to help you set SMARTER goals in your chosen domain.

1. **Choose a domain.** Consider the four domains of life above. Which one do you wish to set a goal in? Consider which one you sense is out of alignment with how you wish it to be. If you're not sure, give a score out of 10 for each domain, with 0 = not at all how you wish it to be to 10 = you feel this domain is flourishing and in alignment with your values. If you're still not sure which one to pick, choose one at random for now.

2. **Write down your key values in that domain.** You can have one or several values that fit each domain for you. For example, if it's leisure,

maybe your values are creativity, curiosity and trying something new. Writing your values down often helps in the success of this exercise.

3. **Write down a long-term goal** you wish to achieve in this domain, that aligns with your values. So, perhaps you wish to play golf regularly with friends, but you currently don't even know how to play golf. So your values in this domain are creativity, fun and certainly trying something new. It also involves connecting with new friends, which you recall is also a value of yours. That's good – your goal is in alignment with your values.

4. **Set a small goal you could do today that links with the SMARTER approach.** In this example, you might decide you will search for golf classes in your local area on Monday morning at 9am. You then put it in your diary to ensure you don't forget. You might also decide to check in with yourself and reflect every Saturday morning at 9am to see how you are progressing with this goal. In fact, you might decide to check in with *all* your meaningful goals each Saturday morning and call it 'SMARTER Saturday'!

So, that's the SMARTER approach. The reflection part of the 'SMARTER' system of goal setting is particularly important. You won't always achieve all your goals, but if you reflect on your progress each time you set a new goal, you'll be more and more likely to succeed over time as you'll keep adapting and changing your approach. If you don't achieve your goal, one solution can be to set an even small goal to begin with.

But…

Does setting goals feel too rigid for you? Do you feel as if you'd prefer to be more vague and unclear in your approach? If being unclear about your goals works for you, go ahead and use that approach. However, if you find that having a vague idea of what you wish to do results in you drifting through life in a frustrating way, try the approach I've shared. Being clear about your meaningful goals doesn't mean they will happen exactly as you imagine – life doesn't work that way. But clear goals give you a sense of purpose, direction, energy and meaning, and each success reminds you that you're doing the best you can to move forward in your life.

JOKE

Wannabe Scarecrow
My goal is to be a scarecrow.
Outstanding in my field.

Part 3

ACT in Everyday Life

In this final part of the book, we explore how to make ACT part of your daily routine, and how to overcome the inevitable barriers that come up when practising your flexibility skills.

This part brings the whole ACT model together so you understand how the six flexibility skills can help you get unstuck and live a more meaningful life.

You'll also discover some key ACT exercises you can put into practice in your everyday life. In this way, the ACT flexibility skills become a powerful ally – supporting you on your journey towards a flourishing life.

15.

ACT in Three Ideas

It's all very well reading this book and trying the ACT exercises, but what about real life? Is this stuff really practical? How can you remember it all?

I have a solution for you. Just remember the word 'POEM':

Present = Be present in the here and now
Open = Open up to your inner experiences
Engage **M**eaningfully = Take action in a meaningful way

So, every time you're faced with a challenge, you can ask yourself:

- How can I **be present** in this moment and curiously see things from a wider perspective?
- How can I gently step back and compassionately **open up** to my thoughts and feelings just as they are, so I can move forward in my life?
- How can I **engage meaningfully** right now in a way that aligns with my values?

This is a great little exercise to do whenever you're dealing with tricky thoughts and difficult feelings. And it can be used any time you feel disengaged, confused or just not sure what to do next. You may find it works even better when combined with an exercise that helps you to be mindfully present in the moment, such as the exercise described in Chapter 12.

Be Present

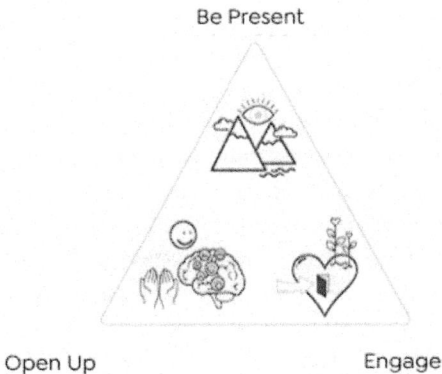

Open Up   Engage

STORY The Walking Executive

I once heard about a high-powered executive who had lots of important meetings throughout the day.

He always made sure he had a few minutes spare before and between meetings – a time when most other colleagues would be checking emails and reading slides or reports. But this guy was different.

Rather than spending the extra time preparing, he just walked, connecting with the sensations of his feet on the floor and opening up to the feelings that came and went within him. When he noticed the chatter of his mind trying to plan and worry, he refocused on his present-moment experiences.

By the time he reached his next meeting, he'd totally let go of any concerns about his last meeting or worry about the one to come. Instead, he was fully present in the meeting he was in. In this way, he found he made much better decisions and was able to deal with any conflicts calmly. Frantically preparing for each meeting wasn't necessary. The best preparation was to be open, present and engaged with meaning. That's a great example of ACT in action.

Is there a way you could integrate a bit of presence, openness and meaningful engagement into your everyday life? Perhaps a daily walk, a mindful shower, some conscious stretches or really being present for at least one meal per day? Choose an activity you could do with full presence and openness – one that you'd find meaningful

JOKE

The Earth is Flat!
My flat-earther friend decided to walk to the end of the earth to prove it's flat...
Eventually, he came around.

16.

Taking ACT Step by Step – Literally

Sometimes, the thought of doing all these ACT exercises may seem too much. And sometimes you're so busy, you can't imagine stopping to be mindful. What could you do in such a situation?

You can simply turn your attention to your feet on the floor. Many people recommend feeling the sensation of your breath. That's great, but it's not always easy to feel your breathing – such as when you're talking to someone, for example. But you can always feel the sensations in your feet, in almost any situation – like the walking executive in Chapter 15.

If you want to develop more flexible attention, start by feeling the sensation under one foot, then the other foot and then both feet together at the same time. This simple exercise of feeling the sensation under one foot, then the other, and then both, has been found in research to have a profound effect if practised for a few minutes every day.

Feeling your feet while you're walking from place to place is a great habit too. You'll be establishing your skill of staying present. Walking a little more slowly helps with being present.

And if you can't feel your feet for whatever reason, feel the weight of your body on a seat or your back against the chair. If you use a wheelchair, you could connect with the touch of your hands as you move around. Find a bodily sensation that's grounding and centring for you. This sensation can then become like an anchor for you, one that gently brings you back into the present moment and gives you a soothing place to rest your attention throughout the day.

ACT Exercise – One Small Lantern is All

METAPHOR You Need

Read this metaphor slowly and try and imagine you are in this situation. Allow the feelings that would come up if you were in such a situation to arise in you. And notice the thoughts that pop up for you too.

Imagine you need to walk from one village to another, which is several miles north of where you live. You have to do this to get some vital medication for someone. A life-saving medicine. But it is night-time and pitch dark. There are no lampposts, and all you have is a small torch with a good battery.

How would you feel? Take a moment to notice the feelings coming up.

What would your mind be saying? Again, listen to the automatic thoughts that spontaneously pop up in your mind in this scenario. What are they saying?

Perhaps these thoughts are something like: 'It's too dark… how can I walk all these miles with just this tiny torch? What if X-Y-Z happens?' Or maybe some other thoughts.

Now imagine that, as you start to walk, a wise woman passing by says to you:

'Don't worry, you don't need a light to shine on your whole path. You just need a light strong enough to light up your next step. You can only walk one step at a time. Just make sure you walk in the direction of the North Star, which is shining clearly. Move step by step, and you will be there by sunrise.'

What does your mind say in response to that? Listen in. But rather than accepting your thoughts as being facts, let your thoughts come and go like the clouds come and go in the sky. After all, your friend really needs this medicine. Remember that you can choose to move your feet no matter what your mind says.

In the same way, you may feel unclear about your exact path in life. But the torch can light the path of the here and now, starting with the very next activity you need to do. Ultimately that's all you need, because you only ever need to take one step at a time.

Which values are your North Star? Can you make space for the thoughts and feelings that come up for you as you walk forwards in life?

17.

The ACT Choice

You can be creative with ACT and apply the flexibility skills however you wish. One simple model you can use is what I call the 'ACT Choice'.

The ACT Choice says that when you are awake and present, there are only two choices you can make in life – living in line with your values or living out of alignment with your values. And as you discovered in Chapter 5, focusing on avoiding, fighting or suppressing your thoughts and feelings rather than focusing on living your values can lead to more rather than less suffering.

For example, let's say being healthy and exercising daily is in line with your values. And you're currently on your computer watching movies. You're low on energy and your mind is saying 'just relax some more', but instead you snap out of your autopilot mode. You know a bit of exercise will give you energy. In that moment, you have a choice. To turn off the computer and put on your walking shoes, or to watch another movie. That's the ACT Choice.

If you manage to make the right choice for you, well done! You've taken a step towards what matters to you.

But what if you don't make the right choice? That's when you need to apply two things – self-compassion and understanding. Do your best to take a few deep breaths and focus your attention back on the here and now. And understanding is about realising the many reasons why you may have made the unhelpful choice. Maybe you were tired. Unmotivated, perhaps? Or just hungry, tired or feeling overwhelmed with boredom.

Learning to forgive yourself and understand why you behave the way you do is a step towards freedom. ACT isn't about being perfect – it's about taking small steps in the direction that matters to you, and understanding and forgiving yourself when you don't. That's just as important.

Here's another example. Let's say your partner is in a bad mood. They say something irritating to you. You feel anger rise up and your mind says something unkind, which you could easily shout back. But you value loving relationships and you know arguing won't help. If you consciously choose to act in line with your values, you might instead take a deep breath and say something to defuse the situation, or even step out of the room, drink some water and come back in a calmer state so you can respond in a more meaningful way.

When your mind is in autopilot mode and you're focusing on running from or fighting your tricky thoughts or feelings, you can end up making choices that move you away from the kind of person you wish to be. It's understandable – living your values can mean facing up to some tricky feelings. It can feel hard in the moment. However, it's often fulfilling in the long run.

So please do remember, we are all human. We can't live our values all the time. We all do things to escape from time to time – watching movies, having the odd drink or spending hours in bed. But if most of your time and energy is spent avoiding rather than living your values, you may want to correct the balance, using the six flexibility skills of ACTION, as outlined in Part 2, to help you.

METAPHOR ACT Exercise – Driving in the Rain

Read this story slowly, and once you've finished, consider if there's any meaningful action you need to take in your life, that you've been avoiding. Consider how avoiding taking this meaningful action may be causing you suffering. Finally, decide if you wish to take a tiny, courageous step that would be meaningful for you.

Imagine you really want to see your friend. Friendship is a value of yours. And you need to drive to visit your friend. You start driving and it begins raining… heavily. And there's another problem – the roof in your car has started to leak.

You have a choice – you can either stop and wait for the rain to stop, or slowly and mindfully keep going. It's safe to drive – you just need to be focused, drive slowly and use your wipers! And you need to accept that you'll get a little wet.

What do you do? What feelings arise? What thoughts does your mind generate?

If you choose to stop driving, the car roof keeps leaking. You might decide to sit in the back to prevent yourself from getting wet, but then it starts leaking in the back too. You end up squashed in the corner – all your focus is on avoiding the rain rather than driving to your friend's house. How might that make you feel?

If you're focused on avoiding difficult feelings or thoughts, it's like waiting for the rain to stop before you can continue to drive. Sadly, you could be in for a long wait. And you'll miss out on seeing your friends, your family and doing what matters most to you.

ACT suggests a better approach is to keep driving, but to drive slowly and consciously. Yes, you may still get a bit wet if your car leaks. But you never know – it may stop raining and you'll get to see a rainbow! But whether it continues to rain or not doesn't matter. What matters is you get to visit your friend.

18.

Making ACT a Habit

Most of our lives are governed by habits. Therefore, if you wish to make the flexibility skills part of your everyday life, you need to turn the insights and exercises I've shared with you into habits.

The following four ingredients are the keys to creating effective habits:

1. **Prompt** – using something to remind you.
2. **Small action** – starting with 10 seconds is great!
3. **Motivation** – having a desire to cultivate the habit because it's meaningful.
4. **Celebration** – rewarding yourself by celebrating in a small way can feel uplifting and help accelerate habit-forming.

For example, imagine you want to create the habit of reading part of this book on ACT every day. You could start by placing the book where you can see it, such as on your bedside table. Seeing the book is your **prompt.**

Decide on a **small action,** such as reading a minimum of one line a day! Something that can easily become a habit you can build from over time. You can read more than a line if you feel inclined, but even just reading one line is good enough.

Reading one line a day may seem like a tiny action, but the action needs to be really small. Why? Because us humans have less **motivation** than we think, especially when we forget our values. By keeping our habit-forming actions small and regular, we are much more likely to succeed. Each time you achieve success, it shows you that you can do it, so you're more likely to keep taking action until it becomes a habit.

Reminding yourself of your values can help with motivation too. You may be reading because it lines up with your value of learning something new. If that's genuinely a value of yours, it'll help you to keep your habit on those tough days and make your actions feel meaningful.

Finally, consider doing a mini **celebration**. Why? The pleasant feeling helps the habit to form. But how do you do a mini celebration? Simply smiling at your success can work wonders! Or you could say, 'Yes, I did it!' or even do a mini-celebratory dance. Whatever makes you feel good in the moment will help wire the actions into a habit in your brain. You don't need to do these mini-celebrations forever – just for the first week or so as you're building the habit. After that, you can let the celebration go (unless you find it beneficial or enjoyable).

Be kind to yourself when you don't manage to stick to your habit. Make a small adjustment and try again. Beating yourself up for not sticking to your habit is not only unpleasant, but it also lowers your overall motivation even further. There is great strength in self-kindness and experimenting with different habits until you find the right ones for you. Everyone's different.

Using Small Habits to Go from Struggle to Success

I've been a mindfulness teacher for 20 years, but I've always found making mindfulness meditation a consistent daily habit a challenge. Being mindful is certainly one of my values and is meaningful for me. I would manage a few months in a row, but then somehow, suddenly, really not feel like meditating, usually because I'm tired or sick. I'd get hooked to thoughts like 'I really don't feel like meditating', and then I would break the habit for a month or more before I managed to start again. I felt frustrated with myself when this happened.

Then I discovered the power of small habits. Now, I have a much simpler habit that I can commit to, no matter how low my motivation and how I'm feeling. Here's my formula:

1. **Prompt:** Waking up in the morning and sitting up in bed.

2. **Small action:** I commit to taking one full mindful in and out breath.

3. **Motivation:** Mindfulness is one of my values and I do want to practice being mindful every day.

4. **Celebration:** I smile and think how I've made a small step towards being more mindful and kindful.

Ever since I've done this, I've managed to keep the habit for much longer. I usually end up meditating for longer than one breath most days. But from time to time, I go back to just one breath. I'm able to do this even if I'm feeling very tired or unwell. That keeps the roots of my daily habit nourished with some mindful watering every day.

19.

ACT and Self-Compassion

The root meaning of the word compassion comes from the Latin, meaning 'suffer with'. But it's not just about suffering. When you have compassion for someone, you kindly meet them where they are suffering, and you offer support, if you can, to help them overcome it.

Self-compassion is the act of being compassionate to yourself, which means to meet yourself with kindness and care and help yourself overcome any suffering you're going through.

Self-compassion is integral to ACT. In fact, developing all the flexibility skills can help you become more self-compassionate. You're being consciously present from a healthy and caring sense of self, you're being open and accepting of your thoughts and feelings, and you're taking meaningful action. These are all acts of compassion.

Remember to develop all the ACT flexibility skills with kindness. Don't use excessive force. Be gentle in your approach.

When I first learnt ACT and began to be clearer about my values, I beat myself up when I didn't take action based on my values. That wasn't very self-compassionate. For example, my work would be meaningful to me, but sometimes I felt too tired to do my work and started getting hooked to thoughts where I called myself lazy, weak or inadequate.

Eventually, I caught myself doing this. I realised being harsh on myself wasn't in line with my value of self-kindness. A much more meaningful approach was to do my best to act on my values, but to be kind to myself when I didn't. In this case, I could practise my value of self-kindness, forgive myself and try again at another time.

Many of us have been taught growing up that we need to be hard on ourselves to motivate ourselves. But take a moment to think about this – if someone harshly criticises you, do you feel motivated or deflated? Feeling deflated (or perhaps angry) is how many of us respond to harsh criticism – we are rarely energised or excited it. The same happens when you are hooked to thoughts that are harsh towards yourself – you may feel deflated and unmotivated rather than inspired and encouraged.

Being kind to yourself is the fastest and most effective way to encourage yourself. Try using your cognitive defusion skills to deal with unhelpful, self-critical thoughts when you notice them.

The Three Steps of Self-Compassion

Imagine seeing someone homeless on the street, out in the cold. To feel and act compassionately, what needs to happen? First of all, you need to be present. You need to notice that he's there, out in the cold, with nowhere else more comfortable to sleep. He has to sleep outside.

Secondly, you need to see the situation from his perspective. What would it be like to be there, on the street, cold and without a home? What could he be thinking and feeling out there?

And finally, you need to take some meaningful action. You may look him kindly in the eyes to acknowledge his humanity, you may give him some money or buy him a warm meal, or you may simply chat with him. You may even decide to support a local homelessness charity, either financially or by volunteering your time.

Self-compassion is turning that same process on yourself when you're going through a hard time. Whether your personal suffering is small or great, you can meet it with compassion.

Firstly, you need to be able to notice that you're going through a hard time. You need to be able to notice you're feeling low, anxious or angry, for example. Sometimes we are so stuck on autopilot, we don't even notice what we're thinking or feeling.

You then need to be able to see things from a different perspective or angle. You need to be able to step out of yourself and get a sense of how you are and how best to treat yourself.

And finally, you need to meaningfully do something to care for yourself. Something that soothes you or energises you, while making space for your feelings and unhooking from your thoughts.

JOKE

Friendly Fruit
What's the kindest fruit in the world?
Compassion fruit.

ACT Exercise – Self-Compassion

Here's an exercise you can do to practise the three steps of self-compassion. Try it several times if you find you have a strong self-critical voice within you, and then try using it in a real moment of difficulty in your life. You can do it in a few minutes or less.

1. **Present and open.** Bring to mind a difficulty you're going through – a difficulty that you feel ready to work with right now. Allow yourself to immerse your thoughts in this challenge. Make space for the feelings that may arise, even though they might be unpleasant. That's okay. Be present to your own feelings of suffering. Notice where you feel the difficult feelings in your body. Notice if each feeling has a physical shape. If it had a colour, what colour would it be? What's the exact size? And the exact location of this sensation in your body? Make space for these thoughts and feelings so you can be in the present moment with them as best you can.

2. **Perspective.** Step out and look at yourself from a different perspective. What words of encouragement can you give to yourself? Perhaps you can try these words: 'This is hard… this too will pass… take it easy as you feel this… take some deep breaths… I feel for you.'

3. **Take meaningful action for yourself.** Take action based on your values to care for yourself. For example, you might do something creative that's

soothing, learn something new or talk things through with a friend. Or perhaps take a short break from your work, stretch your body or massage your hands. You could even actively say words of kindness to yourself. Do what is meaningful and caring for you.

20.

Overcoming Barriers

Two common challenges tend to come up when people put ACT into practice. Either they don't actually do the exercises, or they feel ACT 'didn't work' as they still experience stress, anxiety, depression or whatever they wanted to eliminate. Let's consider each of these challenges in turn.

Not doing the exercises: There are many exercises you can do in ACT, from simply taking one conscious breath through to journaling, reflecting on your values, setting goals and taking meaningful action. This introductory book includes some exercises, but there are many more you might like to try in the future.

Why bother with the exercises? The exercises turn theory into practice. Think of the words in this book – the theory – as describing what an apple tastes like. When you practise the exercises, it's more like actually eating the apple – which is much more valuable and delicious!

When you take the time and make the effort to do the exercises, long-term meaningful change is possible. Start small and practise your favourite exercises to begin with. Little and often is the way.

Expecting difficult experiences to disappear after doing some ACT: We have much less control over our thoughts and feelings than we realise. What we can change is our relationship to those thoughts and feelings. That's what ACT focuses on – not on changing your thoughts and feelings, but on helping you take action on what matters while kindly making inner space for your difficult thoughts and feelings to come and go, which is a far more realistic goal than eliminating the thoughts and feelings you don't like.

The more you focus on getting rid of difficult feelings, the more problems they are likely to cause you. It's a bit like trying to run away from your own shadow – you can't do it and so you end up worn out.

The more you focus on doing what matters most in your life, the less likely your thoughts and feelings will cause issues in the long run. And you'll probably feel more fulfilled too. This can be a much kinder approach that you can achieve.

So try to drop all expectations of getting rid of your so-called 'negative' thoughts or unpleasant feelings. ACT is about making peace with these inner experiences and living your life as you'd love to live it.

Find Time to Sharpen the Blade

METAPHOR

A man was once harvesting his crops. He had to do it by hand. He worked many hours every day and found the work really tiring. Every day he was working harder and harder, and cutting the crops was taking longer and longer.

A wise woman passing by looked at his blade and said, 'Your tool is so blunt! You need to stop and sharpen it. Then you'll be able to harvest your crops much more easily and have more time to rest, too.'

The man replied, 'I don't have time to stop and talk! I'm way too busy and have too much work to do.'

Be careful with the excuse of being too busy to do the ACT exercises. By taking a few minutes to put the theory into practise, you are sharpening the blade of your mind, and you'll be better able to live a more fulfilling and efficient life and make space for what matters.

JOKE

> **Forrest Gump**
> What's Forrest Gump's favourite password?
> 1Forrest1

21.

A Meaningful Life: Bringing it All Together

Humans don't have it easy. Our thinking has evolved very recently from an evolutionary perspective. Although it's been great for us to communicate more effectively with each other and develop smart technologies, these have major shortcomings too when left to run wild.

As a human, you're bound to face unpleasant thoughts and feelings. The solutions your mind gives you to get rid of your negative thoughts and painful feelings doesn't work in the long run. If you try to fix your unhelpful thoughts by pushing them away, you may find they get stronger. If you try to avoid difficult feelings by fighting them or distracting yourself, you could find yourself living a frustrating life, and all the while the difficult feelings grow stronger.

However, ACT offers a radically different approach. Rather than trying to solve the problem of having uncomfortable inner experiences, what if you make space for them and focus your energies on living a rich, exciting and meaningful life instead?

The science of ACT has discovered that it's helpful to see yourself as beyond your mind. From that wiser and more caring perspective, you're better able to step back from your thoughts, accept your feelings and focus your attention on cultivating a life worth living, one tiny meaningful step at a time. You can take refuge and consider your transcendent self as a safe haven, observing your thoughts and feelings and yet separate from them. And if you are spiritually inclined, you can think of your transcendent self as a source of all peace, stillness and love – one that is untouched by the inner and outer storms of life. A quality that all living beings share and that connects us all together.

Flexibility is at the heart of ACT, so feel free to apply what works for you. And if you find that some of the exercises don't work for you, you can of course drop them. The more you can make the ACT exercises yours and meaningful to you, the more you're likely to find them useful for living a flourishing life.

JOKE

> **That's So Meaning-fun**
> Did you know that the Hokey Pokey can give you the meaning of life?
> 'Cause that's what it's all about'

I hope you have found this book a helpful investment of your time and I am grateful you chose to spend your time learning ACT with me. See the resources section of this book if you'd like to find out more and continue your studies.

METAPHOR The Leaky Boat

Imagine you're the sailor of a boat. And your boat has been leaking for years. Your annoying passengers keep telling you to empty the water from the boat using different buckets that they recommend. None of them work for long.

Eventually, someone studying ACT asks you, 'Have any of these buckets worked long term?' 'No,' you admit, sadly. 'The boat always refills with water.' Your ACT friend asks, 'Would you be willing to try something radically different?' You feel scared but you're so fed up, you agree.

She says, 'Leave the water in the boat. A small amount of water is perfectly normal. That water never sinks these boats. The water is just a small inconvenience you have to accept as part of the journey. And after a while, it's quite nice to have some cool water on your feet as you're sailing! It's a reminder that you're sailing and making good progress.'

She asks you, 'Where do you really want to go?' You say islands like Hawaii. 'Hawaii is one destination, but even when you get there, you'll get bored after a while. What direction do you like to sail in?' So you decide to sail west, as you love sailing towards the sunset each evening.

She says: 'Great! Focus your attention on going west every day and enjoy each moment if you can. Set your sails. Sure, dream big, but keep your focus on mindfully adjusting your sails, each present moment, in the direction of your dreams. The other passengers will keep complaining and judging, ordering you to focus on the water in the boat. Just kindly thank them and keep doing what matters most to you – sailing west around the world, enjoying the sunset every day.'

So away you go – it's time to set sail towards your dreams!

Resources

Free ACT Course
If you'd like to learn more about ACT, sign up to a free online course on ACT that I've specially designed to go along with this book. Visit shamashalidina.com/act-book

Free Weekly Tips
Sign up for my weekly newsletter with free tips on ACT and mindfulness at shamashalidina.com

Full ACT Courses
If you'd like to find out more about ACT, check out my free videos or register for a course at shamashalidina.com/act

Live Daily Zoom Meditation + Recordings
To join a daily live class in mindfulness and ACT, visit dailymindfulnessclub.com

Other Books by Shamash Alidina

Mindfulness For Dummies – Overall introduction to mindfulness

The Mindful Way through Stress – An eight-week mindfulness course

Mindfulness Workbook For Dummies – A workbook on mindfulness

Mindfulness at Work For Dummies – Ideal for bringing mindfulness to the workplace

Relaxation for Dummies – Offers a very wide range of ways to relax, for mind, body and spirit.

Mindfulness for Challenging Times – A compilation of tips from a group of mindfulness teachers who trained with Shamash

Mindfulness for Transformation – Stories of transformation written by mindfulness teachers who trained with Shamash

Empower Yourself – A colouring-in book based on quotes from ACT

Wit and Wisdom – A collection of cartoons and short stories to encourage a light-hearted approach to mindful living.

Recommended Reading by Other Authors

The Happiness Trap by Russ Harris
Get Out of Your Mind and Into Your Life by Steven C. Hayes
A Liberated Mind by Steven C. Hayes
Tiny Habits by BJ Fogg

Recommended Websites

ACBS:
https://contextualscience.org

Steven C. Hayes:
https://stevenchayes.com

Russ Harris:
https://www.actmindfully.com.au

Get in Touch

Enjoyed this book, got some feedback or curious to learn more about ACT? Feel free to get in touch with me by email: info@shamashalidina.com

Printed in Great Britain
by Amazon